AF249162

The author and publishers would like to thank
the staff of the many museums and
country houses for their help.

Dinosaur Publications

Tricks and Treats

Investigator's Notebook

by Josie Karavasil

illustrated by Hilary Evans

Published by Dinosaur Publications Ltd, Over, Cambridge, Great Britain.

ISBN 0 85122 407 5 (paperback)
ISBN 0 85122 408 3 (hardback)
Printed by Warners of Bourne + London

If you look hard, you can find some interesting things in unexpected places in churches museums and old houses.

This sign on a church near a river in Norfolk, shows how far up the wall the water came during a flood in 1978.

These beautiful dolls, dressed in clothes of animal skins, were made by North American Indians, and are now in a museum.

Horniman Museum

Look hard at stained-glass windows.
This window from an old house shows
a Jack-in-the-Green, a special jester
made on May day to celebrate
the Spring.

Museum of London

Victoria and Albert Museum

You might like to find out what
glasses used to look like.
These are over 500 years old,
and these are about 200 years old.

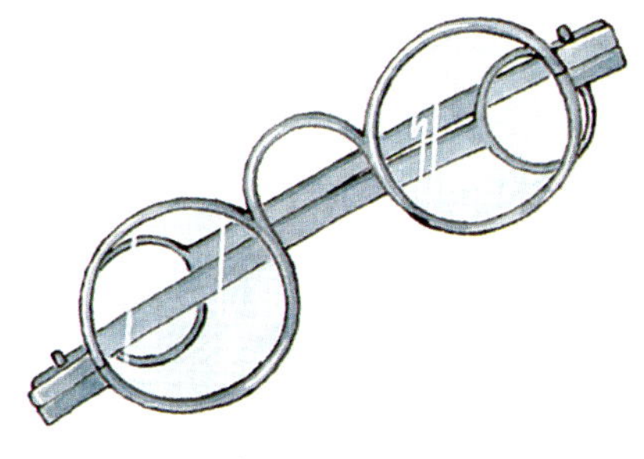

Castle Museum, York

If you look at the insides of
dolls' houses, you will find
tiny mirrors, rugs and chairs,
all perfectly made.

In a museum with a section
for toys and models, you
might see a model like
this one of a butcher's
shop, about 150 years old.

These pots from Peru are called whistling pots. When you pour out of them, the handle makes a whistling sound. They are about 1,500 years old.

Puzzle jugs are fun, too. You had to close all the holes except one with your fingers, and suck the liquid through that hole without spilling any of it.

Birmingham Museum and Art Gallery

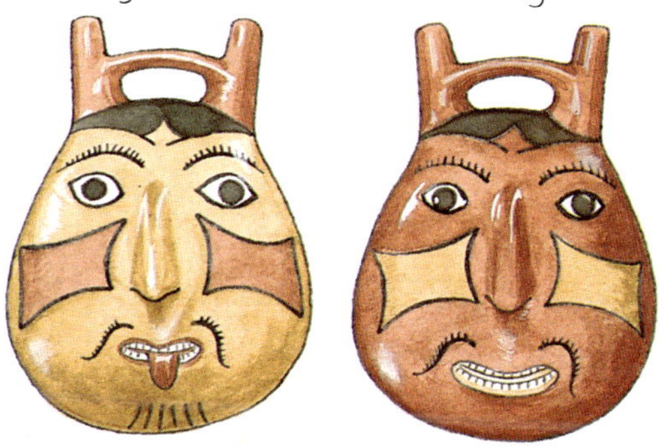

Some museums show what
lavatories used to look like
years ago. This beautiful
bathroom is 100 years old.

About 200 years ago, this wooden
circle was put around the
waist of a baby to help it
learn to walk. It was called
a baby-runner. But the poor
baby could only go round
in a circle!

There used to be playing cards
in the shape of a circle over
400 years ago. There are nine
rabbits on this one.
It is the only card in the pack
left.

Sometimes you have to do some
guessing. Things are not always
what they seem! This knight
in armour was filled with water
and put on the table so that
you could wash your hands
during a meal.

This rooster-horse is really
a whistle.

In another part of
a museum, you might
find a model of a
rich Roman's house
as it would have
looked in the year 100 AD.
You can look in from the top
and see tiny animals' skins
used as rugs on the floors.

Ashmolean Museum, Oxford

Bethnal Green Museum of Childhood

Models of trains often
have whole villages
built up around them.
If you are lucky
the trains will be
working.

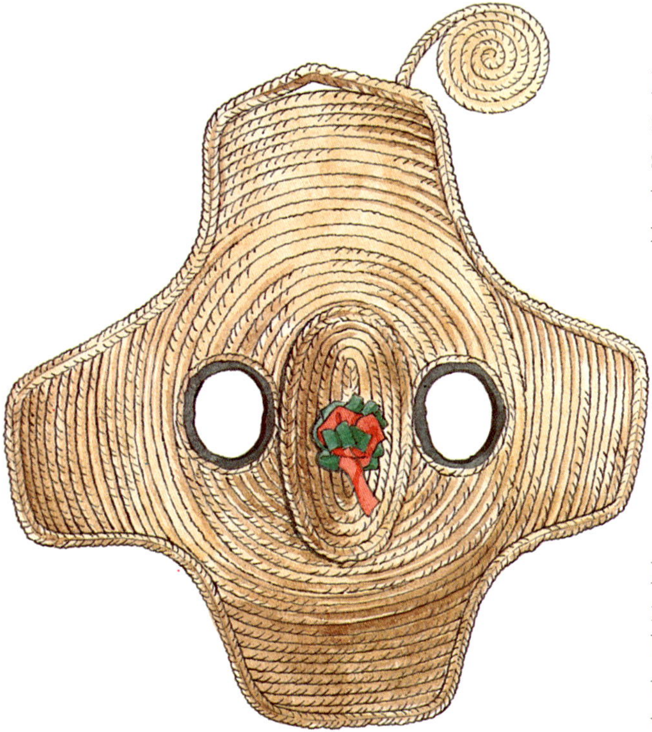

Hats come in all shapes and sizes. This straw hat is a sun-bonnet for a horse to wear to make it more comfortable in hot weather. It is over 100 years old.

But 100 years ago, children must have felt very uncomfortable with this back-board. Teachers and parents taught children how to use it to make them stand up straight.

Cambridge and County Folk Museum

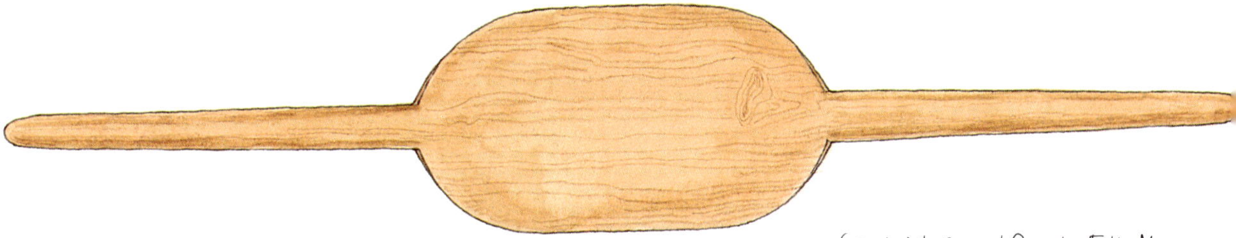

Cambridge and County Folk Museum

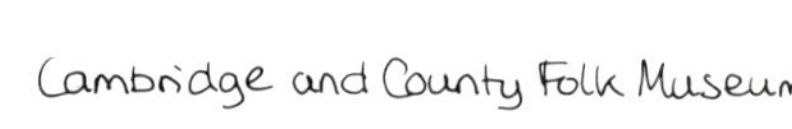

It is fun to search out
old fire engines. This one
is over 200 years old.
It has leather hoses and
some leather buckets.

The Bridewell Museum, Norwich

Castle Museum, York

This one is the familiar
red colour and has
beautiful lettering
painted on it.

Try to find out how people advertised things in the past. This lion was an early advertisement for toothpaste. He has white teeth, but not many of them!

Advertising signboards were beautifully painted. This one, for a fish, poultry and game shop, is about 100 years old and used to hang in a street in Norwich.

Strangers' Hall, Norwich

A newsboy shouts out that this drink is extra special.

Pull the head off this
silver owl and you have
a drinking cup. It is over
200 years old.

There were tricks in the past, too.
Open this box and a Jill-in-a-box
jumps out. She is about 100 years old.

People's Palace Museum, Glasgow

Pollok House, Glasgow

Musical instruments from all parts of the world come in various shapes and sizes. A lyre from Eritrea in North Africa is beautifully embroidered with beads.

This virginal, made in London over 300 years ago, has whole pictures painted on it. Pianos developed from these instruments.

Here are some real North American
Indian moccasins. They are
decorated with porcupine quills
and hair.

A painting of a Chinese official
shows how rich their robes used
to be 250 years ago.

E. Emma Smithson, aged 14, embroidered
her alphabet on this sampler.

The Vyne, Hampshire (National Trust)

From early times people have used mirrors
to look at themselves in. This mirror in
a country house reflects part of the
room. From the centre, golden rays
of the sun spread out.

This very modern-looking mirror
is in a Japanese colour print made
about 200 years ago.

Puppets and puppet theatres are easy to find in museums. Here is a Punch and Judy show about 200 years old.

Looking at clothes and materials can be fascinating. You might find a border of elephants on a sari.

On this buckskin dress an Indian and his horse are sewn with beads.

Look for masks from all over the world. They were used to please the gods, frighten the enemy or celebrate victories.

A demon mask from Tibet

A mask of the Tlingit Indians, North America

From the Cameroon in West Africa

A sea monster mask from Canada

In some countries, actors used to perform
in masks. Here is one from Java
in Indonesia.

About 700 years ago, shadow
theatre began in Java. But
it had been performed in China
even earlier.

Angels and gargoyles peep down
from different parts of churches.

This gargoyle scowls down
from a church roof.

This musical angel used to look
down from one of the stone ribs
of a church ceiling. Can you
see the violin?

Large clocks on buildings like churches and palaces
are often decorated in an interesting way.
The dial of the astronomical clock at
Hampton Court was made in 1540.
It tells the time of day and the time
of year—can you see the signs of
the zodiac? When this clock was
made, people believed that the
earth was the centre of the
universe, and that the sun and
stars circled around it.

This moon dial on a church in Norfolk used to tell merchants when the tide was high enough for their ships to come up the river. Its pointer is in the shape of a dragon. The clock was made in the 17th century.

Smaller clocks and watches in museums can be fascinating too. This one was made over 300 years ago.

In a book you might
find a picture of
a two-headed man
like this. One head
has grown old during
the past year, while
the other is young
and fresh for the
new year.

See what other
tricks and treats
you can find.

Bodleian Library, Oxford

You can find lots of other tricks and treats too,
Why not make your own book and draw pictures of some
of the tricks and treats you find when you are out?
Write some notes about where they come from, what they
were used for, when they were made, and where you
saw them.

Here are some of the places to remember to look:

Museums   Pottery
Country Houses   Models
Churches   Material
Stained glass   Advertisements